Petal of Desire

Divya Singh

Copyright © 2023 by Divya Singh

All rights reserved.

This book or any portion thereof may not be reproduced or used in any manner whatsoever without the express written permission of the respective writer of the respective content except for the use of brief quotations in a book review.

The writer of the respective work holds sole responsibility for the originality of the content and The Write Order is not responsible in any way whatsoever.

Printed in India

ISBN: 978-93-5776-907-5

First Printing, 2023

The Write Order
A division of Nasadiya Technologies Private Ltd.
Koramangala, Bengaluru
Karnataka-560029

THE WRITE ORDER PUBLICATIONS.

www.thewriteorder.com

Edited by Ridham Bassi

Typeset by MAP Systems, Bengaluru

Book Cover designed by Sankhasubhro Nath

Publishing Consultant - Vaishnavi Nathan

Dedication

Dedicated to
The early morning light of the divine.
And...
my rabbit chunnu who had been my
biggest inspiration.
And...
to the "blue-love" of mine that deserves
all the maple leafs of my heart

Introduction

I am not my body, I am not my name, I am not my profession, gathered all this through succession, a reflection of light, in this huge cosmic sight, an empty realm beyond universal regime, just like this, I introduce you to my time.

With Love,
Dr. Divya S. Singh

Reflections

Subtle and serene, and very brightly green,
My heart no longer pumps red blood through my veins.

Enjoying the flow, against many inside thoughts,
This world knows me, in just bits and pieces.

Broke this sheath of liquid personality,
No more stones in my vicinity.

Nature reflect colors in my shades now,
But I flaunt the darkness without bowing
Let them feel me through their eyes,
This life of mine is utterly divine.

My roads are empty, with many twists and turns,
This solitude walks with me, amalgamated with courage.

My cycles of blood shed a part of me every month,
This way, I'm rejuvenated back on this Earth.

Reflection of my petals, incarnate untold stories,
Only love looks red; everything else appears hazy.

Nest

Incessantly and unapologetically in love,
My dreams now depict unusual flow,
Who are you to my soul?
Do you understand what I hold?

Though we lived in that nest for one night,
Our boundaries were drawn clearly and rightly.
Your eyes, nose, and lips made a promise with mine,
To collide with each other, like a million moons in the sky.

You are my hero, my only one of a kind,
Your history has nothing to do with this fresh love of mine.
Oh! Dearest and one and only man in my life,
I am waiting for a hug to melt many ashes into divine.

Your face is full of colorful petals,
Like many shades of rainbow emerging from droplets,
A littlebit shiny, a little bit pale,
As if telling an anecdote of a forgotten tale.

I don't know what's hidden inside your soul.
There is something inside me that values your core.
Reading those thousand poems again,
That my heart has embossed upon your every pore.

But, in my dreams, you stood aloof,
A silence to adore, and still much to prove.
Like that early morning sun, you sparkled my life,
But let this love die peacefully, against my many wishful desires.

A complicated love is hard to sustain,
This I knew when your aura dug in,
It's hurting and aching so damn hard,
Just tell me why this heart is so much in love with your heart?

Broken wings and now a broken heart,
Sitting beside you, I wondered why I laughed!
You were busy praying for the morning scene,
And... I took a picture of the man of my dreams.

I will one day go completely out of your sight.
Till then, I want to fill this canvas with plights.
Take it or chuck it; it's your call.
I'm ready to dive again this fall.

Love, D

Anyway

Even though I am still inside,
And..shattering all love rhymes,
Your eyes keep me awake all night,
My eyes don't want to escape your face's sight.

You are YOU, and I am ME.
The difference my mind knows,
With many unidentified flaws.
But this heart is innocent;
It has fallen in love with your eyes.
How to tackle it, please tell.
Should I leave it here to fall?

You have seen the world more than me,
I'm just a small sapling of maple tree,
Either collect my leaves or burn them,
Or simply sit under my shadow and embrace it.

My little world is full of your tranquil voice,
The charm that you have isn't easy to avoid.
My body has harboured many butterflies,
And this soul is in love with your charismatic smile.

But destiny is my enemy.
I can't see you from my balcony;
You are very far away in this lifetime.
Hold on! My dear, love is beyond time.

I'm small but you are big,
The gap in between us
Is a perfect misfit.
We are apart in many ways,
This love is not blind; trust me anyway.

Love, D

Waters

Standing on my feet alone,
Once again I am stubbornly toned.
Nobody knows my destiny here.
I no longer go to a room full of thorns.
Little bit sunshine, little bit shades;
I absorb heavenly colors,
While singing through every day chores.
Musing alone, withstanding many tones,
The gravity of my words holds many storms.
Wearing the same cloth, I masked my prejudice.
My sword is still shiny, and its edges hates cowards.
There are many judges in my life;
What they control, falls in the category of old rhymes.
Independent and moving, not afraid at all,
My waters are deep, rushing high without any fall.

Love, D

You

23/03/23

Your eyes twinkle like these bright stars,
My heartbeat becomes heavy and hard.

Whom to blame this heart or your charm?
The galaxy of my little life is craving your arms.

You are strong and lively, full of divine light.
I cannot escape you, no matter how hard I try.

You are my favorite maple leaf,
The droplet of the first rain falling on my cheeks.

I have nothing to give you, except this garden of innocent love;
Keep it or eradicate it, you are free to plough.

Call it anything, or give it any name,
I don't care; God is in my frame.

I know I can't live in the nest of your life.
In my next birth, meet me along that riverside.

We will make love, irrespective of the circumstances.
I will be the butterfly, you will be a rose made of velvety petals.

On your special day, I wish you love and only love from everyone's side.
You deserve the best gift, and may God shower upon you the brightest light

Happy Birthday!
Love, D 🍁

Homes

You are a rare flower not born to please.
Remember this notion, it's not at all cheap.

Break these walls, climb up sharp edged mountains.
Don't break your peace, stability is the spine of silence.

It requires grace to be kind to evil.
Amongst harsh edgy voices, you always chose to be gentle.

Forget all dark desires, burn ugly things in fire.
Make no room for hatred, life is albeit short but sacred.

Whoever touches you with gratitude,
Return the favor immediately, but in solitude.

Silence, you know, brings the beauty you deserve.
To pluck the best rose, some thorns you need to bear.

Gravity holds us in many varied forms,
Like the sky holds the thunder, the lightning, and the storm.

My hospitable gestures are now fading away,
They just don't fit in every one's romantic vocabulary in any way.

No half promises, play no cassette of unwind hopes.
This world is temporary, so make no permanent homes.

Love, D

The Women She Has Become 🍁

A little bit dark, a little bit white,
Look how she has absorbed
This color of magnanimous sight.

Living once again, forgetting all the pain,
Her wings are raised for one flight in the mountains.

Made up of fire but, from the inside, a little oceanic,
The warmth of her heart could melt the gigantic.

She plucked those beautiful flowers yesterday,
Removed the thorns with bleeding fingers anyway.

Beauty is one thing she never desired for herself,
So she mended up once again and silently prayed for everyone else.

She knew her worth, left many empty girths;
Her window is open for many birds to chirp.

A colorful face, a mixture of grace,
Reflected her balance, meeting beautifully with the crazy states.

Who knows what she holds inside her popping heart?
Just one innocent word could melt many stones buried inside her since birth.

The women she has become, the one she is becoming,
Holds nothing against this world,
Except flowing against the flow.
She has left nothing to swallow.

That Day

A day will come when you will have to shed your everyday chores and leave.
A day will come when you will no longer have to worry about your finances.
A day will come when you will have to leave behind what is precious to you today.
A day will come when you will have to shed your skin and sync with the winds.
A day will come when the external boundaries will no longer exist in the process of liberation.
A day will come when what you think isn't visible to the naked eye will come and stand in front of you.
A day will come when you will no longer need your breath to support your eternal life.

A day will come when you and this infinity will become synonymous with each other.

A day will come when what you call God will shine and live through you.

Maturity

Maturity, they taught me everyday,
Sucked my air, threw my heart far away.

Who told them God loves false incarnations
Or people who play many tactics with their skins?

Nothing evolves in a confined field,
Maturity is great when you learn it for someone's need.

But, why do they manipulate my heart and skin?
Is there any mourning left to spin?

Anonymously, I emboss many colors on their appearances,
Combined with gratitude, I see soulful faces.

They say they love me for some fearsome reasons;
I hate them but, for no specific reason.

One day my garden of roses will make room for purple orchids
When the bees will buzz without any maturity benefits.

Drying petals tell so many witty stories;
Growing up is a trap, don't eat rotten curries.

Love, D

Illusions

In that well of irksome promises,
I left some horrible zones of magnets,

Attracting me from every corner.
Why do the sun and moon revolve together inside me?

Left some fairy tales, chucked many gritty waves,
I dived deep into this ocean, where the blue water isn't pale.

My horoscope looks nice, come see my palm lines;
Revealing many ages, my skin still shines.

I hit these mountains, piled up in my head,
With the force of courage, I pushed away many deads.

Illusions take my soul in an invincible sphere,
My windows are still open for some rainy fears.

These eyes are stuck on one stupendous scene
Where desires seem confined in one irregular theme.

A dark, empty bucket of garnered emotions
Collect my heart pieces from every direction.

No one is nearby to make this meaningful.
This life is sucking hope from every entanglement.

Love, D

♥

Dream

Overhauling many catastrophic scenes,
This mind is numb but perfectly clean.

Amid these dark white woods,
I searched for everything good.

Those faded visions of my God
Send me messages through many modes.

A decluttered image of a broken dream
Haunts my soul, breaking every extreme.

Where does he live, that little boy with flute?
Why does he sing for me in solitude?

My spirit is naked, questioning many enigmas.
Like a devotee, I sit and watch this worldly cinema.

Everything moves according to his will;
He is my sunshine, my home full of love pills.

Love is way beyond physicality,
He stamped it on my dreamy reality.

Filled my guts, with vigor and courage,
Kissed my soul, and broken dreams were nourished.

Musing with the self, I draw a beautiful home
Where I live with my God, and no one is ever gone.

Love, D

Infatuation

Hey! This is to inform you
That I have stopped writing about you now
because now you don't belong to my thoughts
And my soul; I let you free, I let you go.

No guilt I hold now, no love I make in my mind, no more you touching me the way I want.

My whole appearance is fading, and I am becoming new again.

We had our moment, where we talked in silence,
You don't know anything about my mind's changing passions.

But now, I don't want to think
And rethink about "us."
I didn't know you belong to
Someone else's heart.

You carry on with your life,
I will carry on with mine.
This is how our destinies are designed.

Though your presence still makes me silent.
Your anger makes me fall hard for you
I don't know how to express,
You are the spiritual master of this heart.

But, dear, short-term love,
I want to say,
All happened in my mind
—A misunderstanding that now I can't stand.

Petal of Desire

Writing this to confess again,
As if my heart knows you since ages,
Why do my eyes capture every expression
On your changing face?

You have no idea, how much I craved
One single smear of our souls
Together in a garden of roses,
This love is only divine and pure.

Goodbye. 🍃

Love, D

Tell Me

You don't know how purely this little heart
Touches your soul everyday.

Tell me, is it okay to touch?
Because my soul needs no permission from you.

I don't want to fit in these worldly norms of good and bad.
Love has no boundaries what's the fault of this heart?

Tell me, do you feel the same,
Or is it just a game going on in the realms of our minds?

This love, my dear, should not end.
Tell me if your plans are not the same.

I am scared; your presence completes me
You don't know, in my silence, how loudly I speak.

But you were the one who made me fall
For you;
There is clearly no fault of mine.

What magic spell should I say
To live in the nest of your life everyday?

Love, D

You Don't Know

Through your sparkling eyes,
I have seen galaxies of distant skies.

Through many expressions on your face,
I have seen forms of various sea waves.

Through the aura of your charismatic form,
I have seen divinity as if reflecting from the sun.

Through the movement of your lips,
I have seen stories wandering in bits and pieces.

Through your unintentional laughs,
I have seen secrets hidden in the stars.

Love, D

Dear Valentine

Hello, my special Valentine,
Do you know the reason behind
My many billion smiles
That I carve on my uneven lips
In between the silence of our
Broken conversation?
And, do you know how
I blush secretly everytime
When your name pops up and my phone rings?
The day we met, I was scared
But, now I am tearing myself apart.
Out of many folds in this heart,
Your essence is casting my another half.

Stop me now
Because I don't want any trouble for us.
But what do I do?
Oh! Dear Valentine,
Tell me how do I eradicate you from my mind?

This heart shivers beyond time
When I feel you inside my shine.
I am a devotee of love and everything pink.
I wish you knew why my belly button aches and sinks,
As if it's expecting some strange blue heavens,
Where you and I can attend many sessions.

I know, dear Valentine,
You are now one of a kind.
This love is growing like the purest pearl,
Only for you to collect and keep it in your shell.

I don't want any promises,
I don't want any confrontations,
Neither any bodily fruits, nor any treatment for fluctuating moods.
You are my silence,
You are my little twisted smile,
And that unexpected alien
Who hijacked the planet called "my heart".

Love, D

Confession

Our one emotional collapse into each other
Set horizontal milestones, little hard to settle.

I met you before, but you don't remember.
Synced with monsoons, I denied many surrenders.

Traveled with you, from one city to another,
Didn't realise why I was so scared.

An outdated version of old love is floating in the poems.
My sixth sense says, you suddenly felt my frequencies;

No attraction, no seduction, nothing like that I feel.
The purest form of magnetic pull is driving my senses to nil.

You are from a different space, and will never align with my case.
But why does my belly ache when your name pops up from the cerebrum lane?

Cosmically, I feel the silent touch of your hands.
As I feel the stimulus my heart muscle expands.

What do I call this, some chemical engineering?
Happening without any laboratory,
Should I give it an emotional name
So that love can play its game?

A single collapse into each other;
No physical touch, just blackheads talk.
This heart is making plans
To decide our meeting span.

But I know you are a bad reader;
You just pretend and never read word by word.
This poem contains the stars, for you to collect and keep them in your sphere.

Aware of those serious repercussions,
Aware of my entangled thoughts,
Not sure whether right or wrong,
I am too small for such big forms.

Here I conclude this little encounter
With intense evaporation of heated vibes.
I am writing this poetry as a confessionist;
Heartbroken over a love that didn't even exist.

Love, D

Luggage

Holy like flowing river or some flower in a temple,
My heart holds you still in its chambers.

I pump my blood with divine intervention.
My breath betrays me under your dictation.

I left that city, that air, that water,
And heavy luggage in that corner where you and I stood shattered.

Those heavens, you had promised, faded right in front of us.
When you said "I am dumb", I smiled beneath my skin.

Sweet anecdotes left me puzzled,
Your game was big, but I never giggled.

The memories you left for me to recollect,
Not going to sing your favorite song in Limerick.

You were my shadow and the air I breathe.
I was your wrist watch, without any hour hand in it.

Gathered my courage without prior signs,
I left your anecdotes in the balcony of my mind.

No grudges are left, nothing I hold now.
I am new here, in this city full of rhymes.

Deleted you with dignity and pride,
I wasn't a doll wandering in your paradise hall.

Love, D

Rush

I don't know what's happening.
Is this something beyond my scope?

What's this feeling, controlling my breath?
Where am I heading with the congenial sheath?

My breath is high and disloyal
For one smeary touch of some pebble.

Euphoric rush of many estrogens,
Riding inside with a lot of passion.

Calling my unconditional whits,
My abdomen is aching with butterflies in it.

Who are you to tell me?
Why are you controlling my breaths and sights?

I am afraid but attracted to flexibility
In a river that's flowing in some superb galaxy.

Love, D

Imperfection

Perfection is a high form of imperfection
—One with authority, another without jurisdiction.

Slowly, they grow toward each other,
Through a constant chase of friction,

One shows superiority, and the other is a little less mean;
Just like the two sides of some blowing steam.

Repelling each other, driving but alone,
Their own trajectory is leading many homes.

One shows advancement, another is full of chaos;
Adding suitable norms in many valuable forms.

High erection of fire, through the concept of soul,
A light mindset could only get why we set imperfect goals.

Achieved some high standards
And labeled them as perfect,
But gave up the huge possibility
Of knowing the imperfect.

Hosted many mixed musicals in mind,
Sang many songs with incomplete signs,
And with a lot of distinction killed many hidden divines.

In this process of labeling, we created hatred for ourselves.
We have suffered this perfection to feed themselves.

Lack of clear instincts separates the two brutally.
Imperfection is nothing but some perfection in hurry.

Love, D

If You Are Talking To Me

If you're talking to me and I see a dog,
I will shift my attention from your talk
To observe that dog.

If you're talking to me and we are touched by a breeze,
I will stop listening and shift
To feel that breeze.

If you're talking to me and I see a bird,
I will include her in my sight
To see her wings.

If you're talking to me and I see a flower,
I will shift my attention
To observe its flowery petals.

If you're talking to me and I see a river,
I will stop listening
To question why it's flowing.

If you're talking to me and I see your silence,
I will stop listening
To the reason why it's present.

An oversensitive, hollow, and empty vessel from inside,
When the light touches me, it permeates through my pride.

Apart from this world full of different colors,
I see a world different than the reflection of light and sight.

Call me dumb, or less intellectual,
Maybe less aware, or less informative,
But that's the way I am.

Whether you like it or not,
That's the way I define my nots.

Love, D

Window

The zeal is so high, expanding my dimension.
Like a chirping bird, I play without tension.

My home is beyond the physicality of this premise.
The sky up above is waiting for my wings to fly high.

Encouraging daydreams, working damn hard,
Without resistance my mind is breaking the walls.

A window inside me, growing like a newborn,
Cleared my vision without any mourning.

A little less guilt, holding no more grudges,
The summer is gone and the winter is full of bushes.

Standing on a cascade of thousands of stars,
My soul is beyond the nebular dust and the cosmic scars.

Love, D

Past

I want to go back in time
To fix some horrible rhymes,
And conquer the hidden sorrows
Chilling still in the bone marrows.

I heard cranky noises inside my head,
And took great oaths to overcome that dead.
The duality of the future and this innocent present
Are reflecting my past straight from within.

Holy desires take me back
When I see this burning road map.
Decisions I made, still shake my naps;
The past and the future are always at loggerheads.

That maple leaf I adored so hard,
No more reflects any red-bricky cast.
It yellowed itself and showed my past,
Another year knocking, but why is my heart so fast?

I touched many winter moons with these same eyes.
This vision I see, left many light years behind.
Ghost of the past haunts my naked bones,
But my arteries are full
And blood just refuses to dry.

Love, D

2022: A Tribute

Full of energy and vibrant shades,
More warm flames and less cold flakes,
Hey 2022, you were great!

Like many yearly cycles, you too passed
And taught me some lessons in your classroom.
Hey 2022, you were full of monsoons.

You gave me strength, an armor of experience.
My work place suffered with less grievances.
With all your colors, you brought rainbow in my life.
Hey 2022, you are a best friend for life.

We went together on our emotional ride;
You wiped my tears when loneliness slapped me tight.
You and I lived in great solitude.
Hey 2022, you filled my life with gratitude.

Now that you are on the verge of extinction,
Paving a way for another year to sink deep in,
Promise me you'll return in another year's form.
Hey 2022, I know the transformation is on.

You washed my hatred with your rainy season,
Consoled my mourning desires with maple leaves of autumn,
And quenched my thirst during scorching hot summers.
Hey 2022, you nourished my ambitions with the fog of winter season.

Ageless knowledge garnished with love,
Timeless beauty forever to cherish,
You greeted me with divine vibes.
Hey 2022, you gave me the purpose to chase the light.

Love is real and is always expanding
—This lesson you gave me when we were talking.
Like many other entropic disorientations,
We all are in a constant cosmic rush of devotion.
On my birthday, you showed me my inner light.
Hey 2022, I know you were infinite.

If time is your best friend, then you are the richest, wisest, kindest, and happiest person in the world. ~ quoted by the year 2022

Disdain

Encountered with some blissful gloss,
A heavy heart is playing the same insane noise.
Tremendous emotional filth
Is deposited on my canvas of thoughts,
Encircled by prejudices and religious flaws,
Burdened with many unexpected life shows.
A little less friction between my two toes,
Repercussions of some sacrificed whits
Are taking my life bit by bit in pieces.
Overhauling the same trajectory of desires,
Rolling like a lost stone, and merging into fire,
Many lives I have wasted this way.
Tomorrow is not a better place to stay.
Growing like a tree, my branches are wild.
Sheltering grudges without any pride,
I have witnessed many shattered beams before,
And I am still hoping for some great dreams to roar.
Their constant urge to push me in vain
Is giving me an impetus to rise through disdain again.

Love, D

Seventy Seven

Seventy seven years of a continuous walk,
No regret, no suffocation, no expectations,
This cycle is recharged again to enter
In a new realm of another celebration.

Everything that I left behind, is no more visible to these naked eyes.
But, a vision of hazy likes are waiting to absorb me with immense pride.

The sun, the moon and these stars
—All still young with the same scars.
But there is a difference I want to share,
I carry my scars like many medals of wars.

No cosmetics, no filler, nothing is there that I need.
All the years are beautifully embossed
On my face like many pageants of beauty.
These wrinkles are the lines of wisdom.
In my experience, life is beyond awesome.

They come everyday to offer me love,
And ask about God or anything like him.
Sympathetic notes are played everyday.
I hardly know why we breathe this way.

No issues, no burden, nothing is frightening,
In life's garden only solitude is blossoming.
An achievement I would love to share,
I have passed many exams and am still growing like a student.

My inner consciousness is growing everyday
And juvenile memories are shaking hands like adults.
Immersed in blissful unconditioned happiness,
Death is a lie told to satisfy conditioned unhappiness.

Love, D

Pattern

I draw patterns on the canvas of an empty memory
—I zig-zagged some half-filled dreams there
And erased some with huge vanity inside
To make it look like an honest fare.

Every line that I draw is mere a projection
Of a huge storm waiting for a ruckus to create
Inside a fluctuating tide of emotions; I surrender my every gait.

Against any supportive theme of a white light,
There is nothing permanent in my patterns of thoughts,
Left but some dark holes to show many hidden dots.

Every circle I draw, resembles an unfinished map
And emboss a reality beyond any physical sphere.
In a whole gigantism of enigmatic wishes,
Something is moving very slowly toward cessation.

Drawing a pattern and decoding it again,
My days are shiny in this realm of vengeance.
A wavy hairline structure that I draw every time,
Gives me some blissful sense of why I continue to live in this life.

Love, D

Knowing

Rudimentary processes create suffocation
For young minds; life has ample emotions.

Night and day, they say work and work,
But where is my warrior soul that never resists?

Concrete buildings without divine ventilation
Catch my desires to get some indulgence.

Bricks of bones too shabby to stand by their own;
Many nights are gone thinking about the unknown.

Freedom from the known is another hole
Created to satisfy some inner goals.

But who is free and fierce in this world?
Just one word is enough to blow away millions.

That word is "God"; so fearful yet satisfying,
As if a tune is playing with an authoritative sign.

I wonder why these unrealistic hopes give light.
There is nothing in knowing everything in life.

Love, D

Dead

Manifesting my desires today, here I stand in unison with myself once again.
Rolling like a precious stone, my net worth is not in billions anymore.

A strong hidden force with masculine surge
Is spreading awareness of hatred and love.

Giving myself a little bit calm like a bird chirping in golden town,
Standing quietly without any noise, I surrendered myself for a better future.

An ocean of thoughts colliding with seashore,
Like a lioness, I'm roaring through the core.

A strong magnet that lives inside me
Is holding on to things with some melodies and singing cute lullabies
To let my inner zeal blossom like babies.

But my desires are stuck in
Some dark, viscous and semisolid matter.

Concentrated impact of my blood
Is diluting many redbrick emotions.
So, I am letting this happen again
For a window to open in a breathing space.

Too much dead material is walking around me
That just refused to live in the moment with grace.

Love, D

Who Are You

Who are you to kill me—just anger with a lot of filth?
I play orchestra and die everyday by saving serene tranquil wealth.

Who are you to fool me—just a betrayal with a lot of guilt?
I play hide and seek and betray life everyday by saying things which never tune in.

Who are you to stop me—just a painful thought with a lot of impetus?
I block hurricanes everyday just with a smile of determination.

Who are you to catch me—just a prison with some golden strings?
I capture the sun every day with the zeal of my enthusiasm.

Who are you to finish me—just an unfinished meal yourself?
I destroy age-old dogmas with a lot of hidden prejudices.

Who are you to create me—just an atom without any reverberation?
I create myself everyday in the realm of my imagination.

Who are you to teach me—just an incomplete chapter with wrinkles in pages?
I learn from the stars every night, and the sun is my guardian.

Who are you to love me—just half emotion with some lovely words?
I have compassion for the worst, and give lovely squishes every day to the whole universe.

Love, D

One Day

One day this intimacy will fade;
You and I will become strangers again.

Do you still think that I deserve this full love?
Because one day it's not going to stay this way.

One day, our bodies will not satisfy our fantasies.
Are you thinking about that same date?

How will you deal with that friction?
A question I am giving you as a consolation.

What are your plans for that day?
I am all yours here, listening to you without any wordplay.

A day will come when this "love-making" will become usual.
Our big desire will meet new troubles.

One day we will be out of love
As if strangers caught up in disguise.

I will seek courage to go back in time
And remember our first virgin collapse.

Will you do the same,
Or just want these melting voices?

I am afraid you are promising me the stars
And some half love too this evening.

But one day this love will go like an old breeze,
And our skins will slip into loose sheaths of the time machine.

One day we will be full of wrinkles
And everything will be loose, waiting to be shed.

Are you ready for that day,
Or just want some young foreplay?

I am a vast ocean current,
Drifting in cold and warm spheres.

I am moving on a definite path
With you without any fear.

Our guts will shatter one day;
It's a life process anyway.

Promise me we will end this ride together
And land on the moon with the stars.

Where you and I will be a little less young
And more naked in our skins and timeless scars.

May be out of intimacy and lovemaking,
But never out of our divine true love.

One day we will die, and leave our bodies behind.
Are you aware of that day,
Or just want some juices tonight?

Your promise will pass like these seasons,
But this time I want to settle for so many reasons.

You are love, or maybe just a sweet package of emotion;
I don't know because you are promising me everything.

One day our everything will become nothing,
And our very "us" will vanish.

Are you ready for that day too,
Or just want something out of this moment?

Love, D

Again

Wait, let me wipe my tears and join you once again.

Wait, let me finish my meal to eat with you again.

Wait, let me hear a song to write one for you again.

Wait, let me learn your number to call you once again.

Wait, let me move a bit to walk a long distance with you again.

Wait, let me wear something to compliment you again.

Wait, let me cry in solitude to smile with you again.

Wait, let me hate you hard every day to love you like crazy again.

Wait, let me die fully to live a life with only you again and again.

Love, D

Silence

Witnessed some faces—a havoc scene.
In silence, I gather all my lost weeps.

Collecting fragrances of dried petals,
Wearing a blanket of heavy darkness,
Caught up in a cycle, following ocean tides,
Days and nights aren't miraculous sights.

Precipitating and then penetrating into the soil,
Evaporating and condensing in turmoil.

A cycle so apt, repeating the same wisdom,
Still finding a hole that leads to liberation.

Authentic thoughts are driving my days,
The nights are now a wagon of pain.

Lighter reflection is becoming denser,
Mirrors can feel our similar characters.

Tears roll down through a continental shelf,
And the moon attracts the tide inside me.

A soul with average features
Write a secret poem every night.

Without uttering a single word,
She shouts in silence with great plight.

Love, D

Hallucinations

This head and heart
Are in a constant clash,
Searching a promised land
Away or near.

In my conditioned waves of thoughts,
Steady state of numbness crawls
Here and there to reach somewhere.

But who am I to finish this purpose?
—A question still left unanswered.

Sitting somewhere, but standing here,
Reverberating in two different dimensions.
Ocean surges urging altogether
To live inside and float passively.

But love desires are so stubborn,
Making no way for any little heartworm.

With a vibrant urge to pour myself,
I sit beneath this life tree,
Asking for some fruits and shade,
Surrendering again in great solitude.

Lost love is not lost
—Just some dramatic scenes,
A product of my mind's wavelength,
A conversion of some exaggerated motions,
And inspired by some voices,
Unreal, yet look so serene.

These love definitions, no more I need.
Like a medicine, I am available
To cure some lovely hallucinations,
And fight your hidden ailments.

What will you give?--that's a rude question.
In my favor, stand without prejudice.
Resistance is the key, and desire a lock.
Friction brings life in every moment of flaw.
Beauty is you and me, and not our reflections.
Come along and sit with me
For one more day without any
Euphoric hallucination.

Love, D

Pattern

Waking up and chanting some names
Here on my balcony, I crave for some fame.

A little love immersed in sugar
Calling me from everywhere.

In this plethora of romanticism,
I search for his shadowy gaits.

Unromantic, full of flaws,
His eyes sing a different chore.

This heart is aching so hard
And pain is leaking through many holes.

What's my purpose? I can't see;
A heavy stone reverberating in a viscous stream.

Intrusions are honest desires,
Wrapped with unexpected patterns.

Only lovers could read and connect with
Poems written in his every pattern.

Love, D

Grave

A poem of love, embossed on a grave
Full of white orchids and purple shades.

Some grass growing nearby, against the will,
Pleasurable, holy, composed, and full of fresh frills.

A lost love is growing again,
But in a realm different than this grave.

Wait or die in search of heaven
Beneath many stolen dreams.

A sweet way completing a circle
Full of broken dots, and making no sense.

Connecting them to extract something,
Like a bee does to any flower.

Here, together in a holistic scene,
We are stuck but still praying.

A heaven where there is only love
For all those shedding tears on this grave.

Love, D

Men

This spring touches them
With a note different than us.
They suffer from love too
In a world there within.

I know they love hard,
They expect more too.
Sometimes life takes no care
Of them and they fall like gyre.

They are not what they pretend.
Sometimes more than what they absorb,
There is a serene tranquility that flows.
Full of imbalances, but still floats.

Sometimes possessive,
Sometimes protective too,
But not always toxic;
It's a tough word to use.

They deserve all the petals
—The fresh and the dried ones.
In this world, I know,
Their absence always hurts.

Beyond feminine, a seed of hard muscular desire
Planted by the eternal power
Is waiting to flourish again,
To Live and love again.

We need to preserve this hard side too
That's fading away in an unborn realm.
They are divine and beautiful;
Sometimes more than the feminine.

Look in their eyes and see,
The lashes are perfectly derived.
Encountered them before
In many forms, and still seeing the light.

Only Power is their wealth, is a false notion.
An innocent is weeping deep within.
I have seen it before, and still seeing
—A man only knows how not to bleed
And hide tears with so much effort inside.

Just to escape the identity,
He has to pretend unrealistically.
Injustice is not adhered to feminine;
Dig deeper and you will see
How they have been dealing with this
Without uttering any word in disguise.

This masculine is needed
For feminine to flourish and grow.
They both propagate each other;
Differences destined to merge together.

You don't become any less with a man,
Neither more or something beyond.
It's just a balance that comes
When our individualities sink in one.

Sometimes it gives nothing, sometimes everything.
It's a game of only gaining and not losing
His true self must be preserved.
The need of the hour is to love not to whisper curse.

Love, D

Who Am I

Who am I?
This body or this mind, trying to work together but aren't aligned.

Who am I?
This beating heart or heart's sounds
Circulating the stuff that I take inside.

Who am I?
This thought or this emotion
Making a call in every action.

Who am I?
This hand or this paper
Writing down a few boundary lines.

Who am I?
This sound or these ears
Listening songs and voices so weird.

Who am I?
This morning walk or these legs
Covering each mile, so fragile.

Who am I?
This creation or creator,
Complete but still incomplete
Everywhere in search of something bigger.

Who am I?
A subject beyond this light reflection
Or reflection of something beyond light.

Who, exactly, am I?

Love, D

Little Paradise

Beyond some big dreams,
There lives a paradise,
Small, yet diverse,
chanting some unsung verse.

Full of untouched sights,
Aligning in magnanimous glimpse
As if a valley of sun rays
Casting rainbows through many slits.

Beyond the lights of concrete shells
And fancy cages of our minds,
Calling me to quench my thirst,
This little paradise.

Nurturing me in my dreams,
Washing all the dust,
This little paradise
Is drawing hopes on my canvas.

Love, D

Voids

A wild forest eternally so calm,
Like a lioness, she carries
Her medals of wars.

Once a delicate, fragile dove
Afraid to open her wings,
Look how beautifully
She is breathing
Under a sky full of suns.

Lived in disguise,
Lost the paradise,
Look how graciously
She embossed an oasis
On this sandy landslide.

Like the voids in a flute
Serve a purpose,
She is using her many voids
To tune in with this universe.

Love, D

Flower

Your love is a medicine
I forget to take nowadays.

Maybe, going away from your reflection,
My life is showing signs of dejection.

You are still that flower I never plucked;
Here in my garden you live like us.

Our habitation is one of a kind,
But your little flowery bud is drying.

Time is consuming our nectar;
Hold on, the pain is still in my heart's epicenter.

You gave me everything, I wonder why.
Without any feathers, we were flying.

Don't worry, I see you everyday
Through the cornea of my eyes.

Your possession is way beyond mine,
But you are free to choose, so take no time.

I cannot see you standing like a flower
Shedding petals everyday.

Love is not a slave, but a free chirping bird.
In my garden, there are many;
You can also become one.

Why have you chosen this way of seduction?
Our love is eternal, there is no abduction.

Let me allow myself to pluck you this time
And smell the bliss of your drying petals.

Maybe, this way we can go
To a beautiful world called 'forever'.

Love, D

Ride

Can you come and join me?
I'm going on a ride called life.

We will be our each other;
You will be my only divine.

Some promises we will make,
And strictly follow our hearts.

You will be free to leave
Whenever you want.

But remember my heart is stubborn
And full of unconditional love.

Don't break it until we reach
our individual homes.

No boundaries, no limitations,
Just come without hesitation.

I will make all the promises;
You don't worry, just pack your emotions.

No burden, just freedom
Will lead us to our paradise.

If you lose attraction,
No problem, you can check others out.

My love is beyond physicality,
So in the end, I will be fine.

Our ride will be awesome
If we let our wings grow together.

But I know you are not convinced yet,
And your desires seem different.

Why are you afraid
When I am love and promising you to love?

Come, we will make some memories
And a beautiful reality of our own.

In which you and I will forever live
One more time in a blissful realm.

But, hey! You look worried
Or may be vulnerable.

Love is not easy for you,
I know I have been through this trouble.

But listen, you are not alone;
I am here by your side.

Courage is what love demands;
Move out of that zone and free yourself.

You are mine, and I am only yours.
Ride with me and forget these flaws. ♡

Love, D

Place

A constant urge to merge in one
Comes out of consciousness
Like a rapid influx of desires,
Flowing in a space beyond time.

Sinking me in abysmal depth,
Leaving everything behind again.

Two different realms, but one playing field
Uniting this hour, in a dimension so brief.

Time provides a base, for memories to grow.
Life blossoms always in a steady state of flow.

Don't wish me heaven at my funeral
As I am already living in one.

Both are unified in a constant space
Carrying the weight of good and bad deeds.

These heaven and hell are subjects of minds;
Good for those who are limited on grounds.

Away from all boundaries, there exists
A place full of untouched subjects.

Wish me today, or when you see me last.
A place where wisdom lives with the divine.

Love, D

Form

Waves of doubts arose from physicality.

Everyday, I mourn in silence to see divinity.

Governing me from all dimensions,

A significant form is unveiling the curtains.

A whimsical path full of stones,

Finding direction by itself amid chaos.

Who is lost, who is not,

Nobody knows the plot of this book.

Predictions are raw lies, full of flaws.

Belief is hope with unpredictable clause.

We see what is reflected, and not what is absorbed.

Following minute answers, I beg for more.

But more is not enough, like that form.

Lies look forward, and curse with pride.

When a truthful form encompasses.

A steady state of numbness floats around.

Petal of Desire

Belief is a key to unlock forces so divine.

But challenges are bound to come.

Worshiping isn't any sort of gift.

A prayer reached, but never heard.

Hurdles are pleased with my little efforts.

Something vanishes inch by inch every time.

We are not truth, neither our existence,

But individual universes, with persistence,

Or incarnations, with many aspects.

Our magnanimous self is always invincible

Like that form which is so powerful.

By bowing down to her, some love returns.

A form so serene I could only wonder.

With all my power, I henceforth surrender.

I am her creation, not meant to shatter.

Love, D

Ocean Inside

I see and find nothing.
Who am I? A question comes hanging.
As if a bait or delusion,
Here, the emotions live in unison.

An ocean so rare like the color blue,
Turns upside down everyday and night
Like a poem embossed
By a butterfly on wings.

Tears carry a part of ocean;
A little less salt and more warmth,
Like a glacier melted inside
And rolled down through the eyes.

Nature lives in our various forms
And creates humus of us.
We live in soil, to become soul.
How you and I are then connected?

Manifestation is our desire,
Moving us ahead, hitting with a boulder,
Paving a way for us
To create a heaven out of heaven,
Or may be a diverse realm like the one inside
To surf in the ocean of emotions.

This cycle that we have chosen
Is moving monotonously.
Every tear is an escape;
An open door to a reality
Still left to conquer.

Love, D

Separation

Evening knocked yet again,
But your lap wasn't near, or anywhere.
I slept without tears in eyes yesterday,
Still hoping to see you everyday,
Tangled up in a pure memory
Where you and I continue to live.

'Rest in peace,' says my heart;
A hope so young, but still hurts.
Your eyes, confined around mine
And I could see a million stars.

A molten magma burning inside
Grieving in pain—that is hard.
I'm behaving like a snowflake
Calming down your burning desire.

In all shapes and shades of love,
Different yet beautiful,
You know and I know that
Separation is unreal.

I live inside you everyday.
My place is secured like a locked room.
Your heart beats in rhythm
Whenever I write a song,
As if listening to an anecdote.

Petal of Desire

You attend to my thoughts every evening.
There is no sad part, only a happy space.
You aren't near, but everything inside you is.
Come and make me serene,
I'm waiting for one physical smear.

Love, D

Nothing

Nights are trying hard,
Giving me all the comforts,
Hugging me tight,
Giving a lot more squishes.
But I can't sleep,
Wondering something,
But nothing.

Nothing is happening.
Nothing is going.
Nothing is shaking.
Nothing is blowing,
But still I can't sleep.

Thinking about nothing.
This nothing is pure,
Like God or something.
So still, calm, subtle, and serene.
Beyond any questions and answers.
Beyond any explanations.
Beyond fragmentation.

This nothing is so black,
Like the darkest corner,
Or where no light can reach.
But I can float in a harmonious motion,
Maybe, to and fro like a pendulum.

Oh! This nothingness is full of relief,
Needing nobody's attention.
I am devoid of sleep,
Absorbed in the beauty of nothing.

No pain, no happiness
—A steady state of equilibrium.
Nothingness is my realm,
A resting space beyond time,
An arena in between me and my soul.

No light, no power,
Where the energies evaporate
Such a world is so real
That I daily encounter.

So a message at this hour
My sleepless night wanna convey,
Though we underestimate a power
That is equally valuable
In the world of everything,
I want to become nothing.

Love, D

Hole ●

Cosmic drift inside me is mourning so high,
Like a stone reverberating in deep sigh.

Rays emerging and colliding blindly,
No eyes could see a hole so profoundly.

Atoms radiating without any motion,
The vibration of a heart carries a lot of emotions.

Repulsive acts of misery look attractive.
Without food, an atom tarnishes.

Time and space seek boundless realms.
Opportunities are created in a hollow mesh.

Singularity explains the magic of existence,
A gaseous core and an entropy hidden.

An unsolved equation began in my mind.
A hole to escape beyond, isn't outside.

Love, D

Never Give Up

Who in this world can't write a poem?
It's something hidden in your very geometry.

Look how soothing these skies are,
Like an ocean up there without any scars.

Why do you wonder you aren't special
And push yourself everyday to become vulnerable?

With or without a purpose, it doesn't matter;
Something inside you is never gonna shatter.

So, love your tears like you love these rains
And the sun will rise up for you again.

Don't go by their definition of success;
No money, no fame can buy you happiness.

Look inside, you are already beyond light.
Need no of accessories to charm any eyes.

Whisper something sweet in the ears of life,
And you will unfold many miracles of divine.

Spread your wings and breath high;
Your time has come, just give one last try.

Who is pushing hard and breaking walls?
Only a level playing field is known to all.

And giving up is never your equation,
You need no one's validation.

So, be a beast that follows no beauty,
Live in an equilibrium with all your worries.

Show them your starry dust
And burn them with your fire.

You are that piece of a puzzle
Who can change the course of any desire.

Love, D

Pilu

When I was empty, and the sky appeared less blue,
When the cloud hid the sun
And a storm massacred my inner zeal,
When procrastination took away my breath
And tears weren't enough to combat the pain,
When juvenile love refused to blossom
And trust escaped from my heart,
When they broke me apart into fragments
And peace refused to knock inside me,
When life in me planned to die
And only some sober wits were left,
When hope went in vain
And reality became unbearable,
When I arrested myself in a trapezium
And engulfed myself wholly,
When my mental dilemma carved a scary picture
And everything good escaped with intensity,

You were there, always
Asking about my problems, and somewhere in your gentle voice providing all the answers.
You were there, always
Waiting for me to recover, and taking care of me as a mother.
You were there, always
Wagging your tail to grab my divided attention,
Without any favor in return.
You were there, always
As if feeling my pain, and giving

Invisible hugs.
You were there, always
Consoling me through your innocent eyes,
Against the world you stood by my side.

You were always there, Pilu,
Like a shining star in the galaxy of my universe.

Halloween ♥

An occasion so firm, it took those breaths away.
In some parts of the world, some wept with tears yesterday.

Innocent were the hearts, came to beat the heat,
Little did they know the coming fate was so deep.

A Halloween party, ruined all the desires
Stolen them from the sun, untouched by fire

Some grasped for breath, some mourned indeed,
In a crowded realm, those unfortunate ones screamed.

I am numb, as I can feel their dying shivers.
A coldness is encircling my body at this hour.

So many innocents are now part of the sky.
I pray for a life, to grow there twice.

A cruel Halloween, a curse upon us.
I hereby mourn, paying condolences with a surge.

Dying is liberation, so rest in peace with every emotion.
There is a better place than this, I stand by this notion.

—For the souls who we lost in Seoul Halloween parade, RIP.

Love, D ♥

Where

Where is my mate who was never late?
Am I his reflection, or is he just a haze?

Why am I laughing? Why is there so much pain?
Am I longing for him, or is this lie sane?

Where is my soul who promised me a mate?
In this empty nest, dying is a sure fate.

Who is my caretaker, this food or emotions?
Everything is swelling in deep well of repercussions

Who is my warrior? Tell me his name.
Fighting alone for ages, I need him for a gain.

Where is the sky he painted for me the last time?
Throwing every color on this canvas of rhymes.

Where are the lyrics he once whispered in my ear?
Trying to write everyday some hidden truths, oh, my dear!

Love, D

Tough

Heart is an organ, too busy to love.
Stop exaggeration, we need some tough stuff.

Fed up with promises and predictable lies.
Ample of holy truths are floating in disguise.

Desires are wrapped in beautiful words,
Rotting alone without uttering much.

Slowly fading away, intoxication is real.
A territory still left to surrender, oh, dear!

Leaving again and no one to recall.
This day is blooming again to fall.

Let's together glorify our hidden secrets
And promises we made when we were naked.

Shame is lame; don't pay much attention.
Submerge in a river of some high dimension.

Flexibility is, but, a stupendous hole.
A mundane stream is flowing back home.

We all are monks, in our own world
Preaching each other, silently without words

Love, D

Ambition

Living a dream, unable to accomplish.
Oh! How this love is breaking my ambitions!

Once a free chirping bird,
Now facing an inner jurisdiction.

A huge tide expressed all sorrows
In an ultimate hole, I'm going to tomorrow.

Love comes and leaves you alone.
Suffering is the truth, enabling us to glow.

Finding a dream of our choice is hard.
In this world, funerals don't last long.

Miseries leave us awestruck sometimes.
It's our solitude that keeps us upright.

I am not different from your dreams
Holding you is easy; letting go is extreme.

Come and hug me with all your warmth.
I need one to avoid this cold storm.

Love, D

Who Is Old?

Who is old here, you or these trees?
Or just reverberations in one enigmatic scene.

Who is old here, you or these birds?
Flipping our wings, in the same sphere like nerds.

Who is old here, you or these worms?
Plowing subconsciously, in best suitable norms.

Who is old here, you or these thoughts?
Consuming each other in varied forms.

Who is old here, you or these stars?
Burning everyday, without carving visible scars.

Who is old here, you or this love?
Fluctuating every emotion, with so much curse.

Who is old here, you or I?
Suffering and continuing in search of the divine.

Love, D

What If...

What if I say I will leave you and my obsessions?
What if I say bothering is a past thing now?
What if I say the universe is inside us?
What if I dictate my incompleteness?
What if I say my heart is shivering?
What if I say loving is not serene?
What if I say that intimacy is outdated?
What if I say you and I are liars?
What if I say we are losing our games?
What if I say you are too heavy for my heart?
What if I say I want to give up and rise again?
What if I say give me a job for me to explore myself?
What if I say ugly things are the best?
What if I say heaven is nowhere, but here?
What if I say seduction has no meaning?
What if I say we all are storytellers?
What if I say that everything is only one?
What if I say life is not heading forward?

Love, D

Book Of Life

Today, a desire to forgive popped up.
In mind's bandwidth, it tangled up.

Saving somebody is a powerful notion.
Saving from ourselves is the first function.

We kill many in our heads everyday.
Forgiving is, but, a serene subway.

We list our priorities for them to fulfill.
Nobody is our slave that we wish to control.

Acceptance is not for them, but for us.
We choose our ways to reflect in sad ways.

A simple straightforward message seems tough
In a constant chase of some unexpected trough.

We should accept others' definition of love too.
The world harbors many perceptions to bloom.

Hatred, agony, and distrust come from within.
Why do we blame others in different realms?

Humans are birds and like grass too.
Wanting to fly, still sticking to the grassroots.

Yesterdays and tomorrows are just the first and the last covers.
This book of life is vibrating every single hour.

Love, D

Hope

A ray of hope sprouted again at this hour
When I saw my lord without any feathers.

I can fly too without any fluctuations.
Oh, dear! Wings are just some light extensions.

Chucked some culturally conditioned beliefs.
Look, how I fly without any grief.

This vast ocean of thoughts in my head
Asking to dive deep in search of real pearls.

Why are we so obsessed with solidarity
When there is immensity in varied entities?

You, I, and this flower, witnessed a heavy storm.
Survived, thrived, and blossomed, without any wings at all.

Love, D

Get Well Soon

Illness is not a gift, nor a curse.
Sometimes we acquire it through mischief.

You are atomic, the fundamentals are sore.
Some electron-proton game, you can adore.

But listen, this entity is only half-poised.
It takes only a few stubborn hours to vanish.

Don't decorate this concrete atom everyday,
Pay attention to the immortal that needs no pay.

A cure to all your illnesses lies within.
Sit with this profound kid grinning inside.

You are your own physician, don't give up this thought.
This machine you build, vibrating powers to unleash.

This gathered piece of mass is temporary,
Soon going to become a part of some galaxy.

Enhance this heart to merge with the consciousness,
Chase a dream that reflects some hint of permanence.

You will gain health with the wisdom of the divine.
Let's cross this dry desert, an oasis is waiting inside.

Love, D

Eclipse

Hiding the sun, like a curious kid,
The moon is playing hide and seek.

Today, it covered a shade too serene.
Sun rays are blocked to fall in vain.

The moon with all the axial tilt,
Dispersing desires through many slits.

Rotating, since ages, without uttering
How much it loved and grieved for one single meeting.

The sun meets the earth on a regular basis,
Spread its vibrant rays, for her to flourish.

The moon is, but, devoid of his own light,
Rents it from the sun, everytime with a great plight.

This day when the axial tilt is in one line,
A chance for him to burn the pride of the divine.

Eclipsed the sun for a few minutes,
The moon showed the earth, his love is not light-driven.

Without his own light, he can still love hard,
Convincing the earth, a poetry it carved.

No doubt the sun matters to the earth more,
The moon still has an infinite bond, beyond its lovely flaws.

Proposing the earth without any rays,
The eclipse is still left to fade away.

Love, D

Bumblebee

Once upon a time, a bumblebee fell in love
With a dying rose, in a garden full of lust.

Encircled by flowers, full of adulation,
She chose the one with immense liaison.

Head over heels, in love devoid of any pain,
In deep solitude, she refrained from any gain.

Left her empty amours for a dying rose,
Plagued her heart for some goodwill to grow.

With great proclivity, she impressed the rose.
A mutual partnership for some nectar arose.

Dying rose was nectar-less, soon she realized
Her love never remained, any less confined.

Dying rose, plagued by the cycles of time,
Mourned for his bumblebee one last time.

The bee, however, took an impractical step.
Without any nectar, she decided to rest.

Amid the beautiful flowers, she loved only one,
Whose last petal was doomed to shed.

Love, D

Fairy

Shivering in pain, she stands still.
As if silently, reciting a magic spell.

Yesterday, she fought like a warrior;
Today, carrying a heavyweight.

All the love that she left and burnt,
Rising above through cold flames.

Gently, she carries her medals of war.
Roasted herself, played a scary play.

These things accumulate her hidden desires.
She has a shine, but is unavailable for lovers.

Plethora of lies, they throw at her everyday.
Designed with harsh demeaning adjectives.

Her grace fights back with ample pressure,
Without any infringement or any shatter.

She paints her scars everyday with colors,
And an index of her face with pure valor.

Surviving, listening, and rising up again,
When the sun shines, a fairy dances in pain.

Love, D

Shadow

A shattering shadow, growing in pain
Urging the clouds, not to hate sunrays

Let them grow and thrive once again
Let the soul surf through the ocean of pain

This is the pain that love hides
Without any scars, invisible with naked eyes

When birds chirps, and autumn seek love
Life blossoms without any blowing dust

Shadows are meant to grow and fade
And never afraid to say 'a spade a spade'

Only a brave heart, sings a song of peace
Without any transaction, slowly it proceeds

Some sweet recollections are left to keep.
Thirsty desires of a shadow, weeping in grief

She said to love her hard, before fading away
He denied gently, in his own divine way

Memories drawn on the canvas of thoughts
Some shadows are destined to merge with plights.

Love, D

Repair

A false collision with him this morning
Hung my romantic whits in vain.

Little did I realize, the course and the event
That paralyzed my soul in disdain.

He was but an impetus, following an emotion.
Nevertheless, I surrendered with a lot of friction.

'Who was he?' my heart asserted;
A rosy petal, with a velvety course.

How it all happened, why I grieved.
Unfilled answer, with a subtle breeze.

A window in my heart, is opening again
Is that the same love, or just a half song

The stars are aging like my little hopes.
He is approaching, with dusky smokes.

Amid the chaos, I encountered peace
—A repercussion of some very good deed.

But why in the world do we live with pain?
Because it has beauty, without any gain.

I sit with love, but without his fear.
A void in heart, still left to repair.

Love, D

Autumn

Last year in autumn,
When the leaves were floating outside.
In the night, amid the moon,
some stars were also weeping.
We were together, and there was love.
You kissed my forehead and I went numb
With love and scary turbulence.

Only some dried tears were left inside us;
Sweet tiffs were gone.
Now harsh adjectives took over,
We were merging into each other.
Oh! How beautifully a realm was created.
I slept on your lap
And you wept inside,
heard the sound of your trembling emotion,
Singing in Limerick with mine.

That day I slept without fear,
As my lord was so near.
Your presence made me serene,
Your touch embraced my soul.

A longing, a craving, a struggling heart,
Calling you to just merge once more.
You are everywhere,
And your absence now sucks.

My life is casting a teary rainbow
With one color of our love.

We came and shared our parts.
Only our eyes could see
How charismatic that every aspect was.

But together we were a misfit,
United to build our little infinity.
And we were always living there
Where no time could ever reach.

That's a realm of our imperfection,
So now I am fully awake.
A pinch of your gentle touch,
Pain, grief, and a lot of it.
Going back in those times
To meet you on this earth
One last time.

You are my only peaceful place
Where I wanna live and die.
In every birth, in every death,
Leaving everything for you aside.

Come and meet me, so that I can sleep
One more time on your lap.
Kiss me, because I don't wanna feel
The touch of this appearing light
Which is shining every day
In our blossoming autumn together.

All these years, when we were alone,
I saw it coming every day.
You, I, and our beautiful space,
Fading but with grace.
And,

Is heading toward a lonely death,
To reunite us in the next birth
That we will take.

Love, D

Our World

You gave me my little world.
You have no idea how happy I was.
It's painful, we aren't together anymore,
But together is a misnomer
And reality is an optical illusion.

We had our realities
For which I am grateful,
But in our little world we are
inseparable,
Away from any mixture,
Just purely our souls.

I know it hurts too
That I am still alone;
Alone, but not sad.
Looking back at our 'forever,'
That you and I promised
In our beautiful world together.

Sometimes this heart weeps out loud,
Just for you to listen one more time,
As if giving you the privilege again
To break it once again.

I am going to live like this
In our world that reminds me of us.
Nobody is allowed in that,
Not even you, or your false truths.

I will be forever yours,
This way only, just here.
Come if you want, or don't come;
It doesn't matter till the last breath.

Love, D

Grass ❁

Sitting alone, along with the grass,
Looking at it with concentrated eyes,
Admiring the blades and the watery drop;
The stillness of it made me think a lot.
Can I too be like this—
Without the drop wetting my soul,
Simply static, no more console
With calm, steady flow
Without paving any way,
No rolling, nothing this time
Dropping down at every dawn?

Life is a mundane process,
With cycles moving in paces
I and the grass petal are exactly the same,
With merely a construction difference.
So, my untouched whits told me
To be with this process again
Without holding any wet tears
In sync with the unknown once again
Everything knocks every day,
Only we don't recognize
That with keen attention
Everything is a gateway
To reach the divine.

Love, D

Forgive

My soul, one day, met with the universal soul;
So serene, calm like something divine in whole.
I asked, 'Why did you choose me?'
It said, 'You are like me.'
I was taken aback, in the moment that just flashed.

Years ago, a life was born,
Blossomed, thrived, struggled, lived
Through all the faulty narrows.
In its vulnerability, life was beautiful.
Without any mixture or blend,
A color that was so dark yet sober,
Life threw on the universal canvas.

And now it is dead, but not detached
from the love that it cultivated.
Some, broke the heart; some, broke the soul.
But life was still craving for one last universal hole.
So it came afterward,
Chasing a dream
To teach this gross life,
In the form of a universal soul,
To teach how not to attach
With the plethora of visions
They throw at us, and not flow in the waves of emotions,
Why it is good to be forgotten,
Why should we take the road less traveled?

Life was convinced, as the search was over.
No more it craved any perfect lover,
As now it knew the pattern the universe draw
In the road of every disciple,

And why we all are monks
With our individual roads,
Our personal desires, with philosophies of our own.
The universal soul shows us the mirror,
Everytime we fall apart
In different realms that are still connected
With all the universal holes,
But
'How to forgive and let go things that shatter' is a whole new question
Life asked.
To which, the soul replied quick fast,
'Forgiving is superior, just like God.'

As enchanting as the deepest universal songs,
Only the one who forgive deserves the love
—That's just a single universal code.

Love, D

Butterfly And The Flower

How a butterfly fall for a flower
Is a sweet anecdote
With a lot of mixed juicy blend,
Unleashing the taste of quince
Secretly through their love.

It all started with a sight,
A little 'give-n-take,'
A lot of 'symbiosis.'
Fell for the aroma, she knew no aftermath.
A duty she carried, a mischief she did.
Pampered the petals with everything velvety.
Little did she realize the business.

Flipped some pollen, while roaming in the garden.
How happy she was, she chose the best flower.
Seasons grow and time changes too.
With dried nectar, the flower witnessed a hazy hue.

He knew the time has come
For the petals to shed,
But the butterfly was determined,
Madly and irresistibly in love.
In her innocence, she conveyed her wish
Not to go on with the business any further.

The flower commanded to leave,
But she was determined for a sacrifice.
The love that she bears, like a mother bears a child.
Her heart was heavy, but full
With the only desire to love her lover more.

Petal of Desire

Even on his deathbed, amidst petally woes,
In her buzzing, she uttered,
I shall die wrapped in your petals
Then to live a life without your nectar.
I might end up in disguise,
But my heart will blossom
With your smell forever.
This is my love—all for you.

I know little business, more sacrifice.
No price, no 'give-n-take,'
Just the beauty of dying
Is nothing less divine.
Nevertheless, I will continue
To go on with the symbiotic association
That my wings have the rest of the garden.

But these petals are for them.
They could chop them;
I didn't wonder.
All I know is your nectar and my sweet love,
For which I am willing to
Encounter many falling autumns
For you and with you.

Don't worship me, or my wings.
I am extremely fond of your velvets
That sparked my wings when I first landed
In your gentle loving aura.

Don't betray my love.
Give me some space to die
With you amid the very essence of us.
Swallowing the juicy desires.

A little poison, but a lot of medicine,
Your love has everything,
Everything."

Love, D

Again

A stir the sick selfless heart,
Pondering again
Why you left those words
That made me insane.

Bewildered by thoughts,
Searched your timeline,
Where in January
We were holding hands.

Looked at you, but my mind denied.
When the heart rules, everything else takes a back side.
Peace smeared all over my body
Like I missed a breath so heavy.

The stars knew me more than you do.
They told me not to see you;
I accepted their shine
Not to love you again.

Afraid, I might end up meeting you,
Without meeting my God again.
This love that had shattered my soul,
Recalled it a million times.

But you didn't want us
Amid the moon and stars.
So, I left without uttering
A single notch from my side.

Wept, but with empty tears.
I held myself with fear;

To not to think about you
Was an immense pressure.
Signaling my neurons
That everything's gonna be better.

As I confronted my guts
So longed to be with my happiness
I found a stubbornness
Again while seeing your picture.

Mixed feelings coming
You know, heard that now, you are gone completely.
But why am I hoping
To see your toxicity appearing?

Even for a moment my heart pondered if
It met with yours, somewhere.
Is that your magic or just my old love
That you crossed my mind's lane
Yet again with flowers?

I hope it has never met.
My desires are yet to be fulfilled.
I am still on my journey
To please my inner peace.
But there is a grave too
Hidden beneath my thoughts,
Where I wanna go today
And sleep forever.
Such a winsome love, that seems so far.
Nevermind, your lies are still in the heart.

Pain

Here, I stand seeing my heart weeping in pain,
Waking up, and sleeping again.
I have encountered many pain,
But this, this right here, is
Sucking me, as if tearing me apart into pieces.

I have abandoned all the desires wrapped in pain.
But this, right here, is choking my breath.
It's September, and it knocked again.
Here, right here, beneath the heart muscle,
This time is so subtle, and gentle.

I want this pain;
I ordered it and they parceled.
Holding the ashes of dead, burnt love,
I am covered with it all over.
I want to hold it, until it reaches every corner of my heart,
And let me sleep in vain again
To find those blooming seasons of love.

When we were in the same realm,
Singing some songs
With icecreams in hands,
And you wiping the cream on my lips,
I still get piloerection.

Amid my fiery whits,
I resolve every tiff
That we had, and still have.
But this pain, right here,
Yelling at me, telling me to stay with it.

I am honored, that I crossed you
One more day.,
Amid so stubbornness
I settle for this pain
From everywhere
That my teenage love
Had embossed so profoundly.

The reflection of it from my wounds
Are still fresh like sweet marshmallows.
I heard somewhere, you have found a love again.
I smiled, and could've let this pain go,
But no,
I would rather continue my journey
On with this pain in heart and soul
Until I find my infinity.
Where you and I are still frozen in the time scale.

I bet I will not let go of this pain,
As this is just one trophy of love
That you have honored me with.
I let you go, but not this pain.
One more day in my senses
To not scold at least this.

The fear of losing you is no more
In that scarce space,
Where you and I live,
But you can't take away this pain,
And my virgin soul
That's crawling to reach in that ocean of love
Through the path of the pain you gave.

Who Is He

How does he turn on the light every morning?
How does he speak in the voice of these birds?
How does he sing, how does he play, how does he cry, and how does he eat?

'Who is he?' My heart asks, 'Where does he live?'
What is inside me that tells that he exists?
He is everywhere, in every moving, and static entity.
He knows the universe, the sun, the moon, and everyone revolves because of him.

When I smile, it's him; when I cry, it's him; When I eat, it's him; when I sleep, it's him.
'Who is he?' I ask, 'Is he the one who protects me when I cross the road?'
Or the one who will save me when I go on my journey beyond death.
How can I meet him?
Tell me where he lives, where he plays
I wanna go there and play with him, laugh with him, they say he is very beautiful,
I want to look at him and admire his beauty,
I want to sleep in his lap,
I want to ask many questions,
But tell me where he records who he is.

My days now starts with calmness,
With a void in heart.
My day shivers and nights remain sleepless.

Who is he?
Where does he live?
My daydreams, and night goes beyond dark.
Engulfing in a static sphere,
In a hollow zone where in search again,
I think that beyond this dark hollowness
He lives.

He who is the beginning and the end.
He who is satisfied with himself.
He who never smiles, but himself is a smile.
He who is not visible, but is everywhere in everything.
He who is love himself.

In the love and timid desires that live inside my soul,
I haven't encountered him yet.
Longing for the meeting one more time,
My heart has taken a birth.

'Who is he?' I questioned.
'I am the question,' he answered.

~D

Peace

Inside me an impetus of love is shattering like the eclipse on moon,
And peace is heading toward me from all dimensions.
I encountered your presence last week,
And that made me weak.
But now my heart is shivering to move a step ahead.

You came like a breeze, touched my heart gently,
And left everything behind without a consign.
I regret for having you one more time,
As I know you betray everytime.

With or without validation, you resist your assertion.
But I didn't fall sick this time, as I understood your tactics.
You are merely a dry leaf,
And I don't need the water you left out of kindness,
Or the goodness that you show.

'Leave my thoughts and this heart,' I say this out loud.
Let the peace of August sink in one more day here in this heaven.

~D

Essence

I met you at the platform; you looked nice.
My eyes resisted to meet yours there,
But the heartbeat grew with a smile.
I encountered your hand and shook it,
Just to make you realize that I broke it.

Longed to see you, don't know why.
Craved for your presence, but I lied.
Once we saw the moon and sung those songs.
I still remember that essence
With which you were drawn
Towards the wind and a little bit toward me.

You denied, but I realized
What your heart was saying.
So, there you cared for me again
With that blanket you offered;
It reminded me of how cold it was.
Though in that scorching hot weather,
Wanted to talk a bit more,
Wanted to listen to how you spend your days.

You weren't mad, but egoistic;
I figured it out a bit late.
In the night I came twice,
Just to sit by your side,
And see you like a full moon growing
Amid the stars with a bit of sunshine.

Petal of Desire

I honor you for controlling and being this gentle,
Like the man you are, I fell a little faster.
You didn't realize, my heart skipped a beat
When you came closer jokingly.

Four days after the journey is over,
I am still stuck there in that city, on that train.
My heart says don't fall, but I fall again
With a desire not to get you, see you anymore.
This hurts a lot; you won't get I bet
This sucks inside; you won't realize.

You are happy and contented,
And surrounded by flowers.
I am happy too, encircled still by your essence,
By your essence at this hour.

Broken 🖤

I left hitting the gate so badly,
Pouring all the irrelevant noise that was tearing me apart
Into one last breath that I took in that room.
I shattered and I ran away.

Wondering, oh, once again, how I missed that possible chance!
Counting the stars every night, I haven't seen my shine till tonight.
I ran kicking that door so hard,
Wanted to rest in my mind's backyard.

Puzzled in my own hollowness,
Left everything behind with numbness,
Left the pair of shoes in that room.
I realized that after screaming so soon
In a region of unmatchable frequency,
I left in such urgency; I was barefoot all my way,
Didn't realize this until I got pulled away
With thoughts and emotions making me fool.
Until today where it sounds so old-school.

It rained heavily that day.
Life is just like this anyway.
Why don't you go and say sorry
For being so rude with people who worry?
For you every time to make you better,
A version of you that's hard to shatter.
You should apologize for your every damn mistake.
That you unintentionally made for your sake.

You should leave this attitude of yours.
Serving problems on the table of your heroes.
I learnt this and screamed aloud.
To grieve in pain that made me shorter than himself,
To become the hero of my destiny.

Come on, I won't allow him to be that;
I will break the glass of emotional stress,
And go with my own chaos
In that noise of my voice,
In that noise of my voice.

New Autumn 🍂

Shine and shine when the plethora of dust put up on you,
The innocence base of concrete bricks.
Rise and rise when guardian angels feel exhausted upon you,
with you and for only you.
Choose to be your own miracle just when the stars refuse to be one for you.

This year is slipping from my hand.
Tell me what's more that I am supposed to do?
Above up, there a sky that lives
with its own fearful desires to live.
I got a cloudy home in that sky;
That's a dream for many of you
sitting by my side.

I know, you have safely arrived in the dream which never satisfies,
the agony, the love—there's so much in it.
And I know where it exactly hurts.
Little wishes for my tiny heart,
May you live long, your legacy longer.
May you enjoy the coming autumn
With grills and chops in your hands all together.

My wishes with the family of yours
That lives and survives within you.
May you never give up on them,
Let these blessings be fully upon you.
Chucking all nuisance in some haphazard way,
We all played this year; well, admit it anyway.

Aching all over again, the shadows of pain and coronary waves.
Making the staple diet a keto, for a hungry stomach in that road show.
God is one and gracious for all.
Le'ts pray one second for the creator of all;
He needs blessings, too, yeah!
He lives inside you.

No matter how far the sunshine goes, darkness has its own glittery holes.
My rain is coming soon this year;
I am ready for that, ready for that.
Just close your eyes and the shadows will be gone forever.
Trust your instincts and the winter will be cozier.

In our mutual role of putting up the universe before us,
Let's pray for the leaves and the animals.
May the coming year bring joy for every single being.
I pray, oh! Again, I pray.

~D

👂 Listen

When I say I am okay,
Don't believe that.
When I say things roll up and down,
Don't agree with that.
When I say the sun hit me everyday,
Listen to that.

When I tell you a secret,
Please be good enough in keeping that.
When I mourn in sorrow,
Let me weep with that.
When I wanna swing,
Encourage that.

When I say I wanna end up in disguise,
Hug me tight.
I need patience, I need people who listen.
No suggestions, no opinions;
Just one more time
I need that listening divine.

~D

Loved ♡

Dusky wind blows my hairs,
With the dust entering into my soul.
This embossed an unusual path,
That is hidden like the universal road.
A road that is less traveled,
A shabby path less stalked,
A service less given,
Like a drum less beaten.

Mongering the foster child,
There is still some hidden divine.
And only trust could see and bear;
Our forgotten love is far more real.

Roses and violets tear me apart,
Like their petals I adore you so hard.

~D

Fall 🍂

Gulp the enchantment of flowers,
Make my holy senses turn red.
Blossoming into this feathery nest,
Look how I am evolving.

Lumps and crumps sketching the canvas,
In life's den it's now or never.
Fearsome desires turn hot blue,
I fell in that hue.

Broom of dreams cleaning the dreams,
Shattering somewhere I didn't bleed.
Hope is, but, a word of four,
I shall not stay here anymore.

Oh, Lord! This destiny is straight.
I shall die one more day,
One more night,
One more time in delight.

~D

Fearless

Stumbling upon this road of dust, I know that I cannot see that crust.
Coming, waving me a hand, I don't know where this all gonna end.
I was once a free soul of brass, amid my sun and this grass.
Lying down like nothing to grasp, my holding was so much dragged.

I met a woodpecker yesterday in the woods, tumbling over his skills,
But in my waves everything was curved.
Butchers go together in this.
I heard my grandpa's saying on this.
Onus of encouragement still exists.

Bewildered, but to see who cares,
I settled and asked Robin, are you too aware of this merge?
Robin replied with a yes!
I exclaimed in rejoice as I knew that good days were on surge.
Good days are on surge,
Those good days are on surge.

~D

From Everywhere

So far there, you are gone from here.
Amidst our stubborn senses here,
They refuse to turn down.
But I have no idea for what and where.
You are a smile, I know all that I have.
You are the breath that I know my day takes.
Like the moving sphere and a pendulum, you hit me everywhere.
I have chucked those numb words there.
For you to make my day jiggle with laugh and love and a half hug,
I choose you from everywhere,
From everywhere.

~D

Goodbyes

Here, I stand again
In search of something that's not sane.
I conquered a million stars, sunshines, and snowflakes.
They all failed to keep me one more day.
I came and settled for those words that I never uttered.
I silently walked away from his bare shine.
With a spark of love in my heart, and a desire,
Not to meet him again ever
In this life,
In this life.

~love happens

The Wind

Mourning day and night, this heaven is a shattering light.
I came and was gone for no reason.
Here I stand still, but frozen.
Admire me or detain, your path is the same.

As I stepped out, I became a bit sane.
No more I grieve, not a single drop of tear.
I flow like a wind in an open direction everywhere.
Wind, O wind, come take my live ashes
And blow them with dignity and a little love.
I don't pray, I don't chant this every morning.
Fallen leaves tell a story too; I am listening to one now.
You are my future, it tells, waving here and there.
I am your past,Ii nodded, frozen still there.

~ D

You Write. We Publish.

To publish your own book, contact us.

We publish poetry collections, short story collections, novellas and novels.

contact@thewriteorder.com

Instagram- thewriteorder

www.facebook.com/thewriteorder

www.ingramcontent.com/pod-product-compliance
Lightning Source LLC
LaVergne TN
LVHW041851070526
838199LV00045BB/1545